All Tangled Up With The Living

All Tangled Up With The Living

poems by

Louis Jenkins

Acknowledgements

Grateful acknowledgement is made to the editors of the following publications in which certain of these poems first appeared: *Abraxas, Agni, Ascent, Black Warrior Review, Boston Review, Columbia, Chariton Review, Hawaii Review, Indiana Review, Inroads, Io, Ironwood, Kenyon Review, Lake Street Review, Lake Superior Journal, Madrona, Milkweed Chronicle, Moons and Lion Tailes, Poetry East, Poetry Now, Port Cities, Puerto Del Sol, The Sun, Virginia Quarterly Review.*

Cover painting, *Northern River*
by Tom Thompson, 1915
National Gallery of Canada, Ottawa

First Edition

Library of Congress Cataloging-in-Publication Data

Jenkins, Louis, 1942-
    All tangled up with the living : poems / by Louis Jenkins. - - 1st ed.
      p.   cm.
    ISBN 0-915408-42-2 : $6.95
    I. Title
PS3560.E488A75   1991   91-8259
                                  CIP

NINETIES PRESS

Distributed by Ally Press Center,
524 Orleans St., St. Paul, MN 55107

For my family

Table of Contents

One

Two

Three

Four

ONE

THE LOST BOY

When Jason did not come home from school on the bus Barbara began to worry. She went next door to ask if Bobby, who rode the same bus, had seen Jason. Bobby remembered seeing Jason but didn't think he got on the bus. Bobby's mother, Teresa, said, "Oh, he probably just decided to walk." Teresa thought Barbara was a silly woman who fussed over her children. Bobby and Chris set out to look for Jason. It was an adventure, a search through the dark continent. Barbara used Teresa's phone to call the school. Meanwhile, Jason returned home, went in the back door and up to his room. Through the open window he could hear his mother in the next yard. He flopped down on the bed and looked at comics. He could hear his mother talking about calling the police. He lay looking at the big crack in the ceiling. He thought about what it was like to be lost. He thought he could hear voices, far away, calling his name.

OUT-OF-THE-BODY TRAVEL

Body and soul are linked as in a marriage, a sort of three-legged race team, and are usually comfortable with this arrangement. If the soul is forced to travel alone it does not wing its way over wide water, does not fly skimming the tree-tops. No, the soul shuffles along like any body, eating at lunch counters, listening to conversation in the bus station restroom. . . "Fifty cents? I think I can get fifty cents, . . . " riding the bus all through the dark night, watching the distant, singular lights go past, wondering all the while if this trip was really necessary. Meanwhile the body sits, inert, staring at the T.V., needing a shave, a nail trim.

A PORTRAIT OF THE MASTER

In this picture Jesus stands, surrounded by follow-
ers, with his right arm partially raised, his index
finger, slightly crooked, pointing upward. His left
arm extends downward, palm open. He looks as he
often does in pictures, white robe, sandals, beard
neatly trimmed. His hair is rather long but clean. His
face is calm, unwearied, because Jesus maintains,
even thrives under the pressure of constant travel
and the demands of those who flock to him. These
are a ragged bunch, malcontents, the disenfran-
chised, those for whom heaven is impossible, the
only ones who show any interest at all in what he has
to say. They want help, they come to tell their stories,
to ask questions, but mainly to listen. They have the
sense that He is one of them, only better. And though
the word He brings is difficult, it is the saying that is
important. We must continually explain ourselves to
ourselves. There is no one else to listen. He says
again: "Here is the earth. Here is the sky."

DOWN TO THE RIVER

When Daddy married Mama
she made him go down
to the river and get baptized.
When Daddy went down
the congregation sang
We shall all come together at the river.
When the preacher pushed him under,
when the water rolled over his head,
Grandma said she saw the devil
rise up from the water
and shake himself all over like a dog,
then wade to the other shore.
Grandma didn't say where he went from there.
Grandma said for sure
we will all rise again.

In the yellow light of the room
you brush out your hair
a hundred long smooth strokes
and I lie still on the bed.
What can we do? I ask.
There is no answer.
When the light is turned out
it is so dark I can't see
my hand in front of my face
but it is you I reach out to
in these hard times
no other.

Rise up! Rejoice!
Rise up in the rainy night
like a mushroom from the damp forest floor,
a destroying angel
clothed in robes of purest white,
a simple and deadly life.

Let each day be a day of praise and
thanksgiving.
If you are lost in the forest
eat the mushrooms and die.

This is the river Jordan,
the healing stream,
troublesome waters,
the high wind of the stratosphere
in which the ragged earth is bathed.
I hold out my hands.
These are lands to the left and right,
little islands called the Lucid Moments
completely covered by the high tide.
I wiggle my fingers.
These are fishes that swim in the sea.
Any moment now you will go under
so there's no reason to be afraid.
If someone grabs your left hand
or your right hand
and asks if you want to be saved
tell him no.

OKLAHOMA

On this rolling and open prairie anything higher than
a horse's head is obtrusive and out of place. Grain
elevators and oil wells strung together by right-
angled roads, seem altogether the wrong approach.
Go south two miles, take a right . . . . A tornado
doesn't bother. It blows cross country rearranging
the debris to suit itself. Anything built here should,
like open shelving, allow the wind to pass right
through. Suppose the books fall, someone will pick
them up, dust them off and replace them. Shakespeare,
the Bible . . . there was something there, just beyond
us, by the cottonwood and the dry creekbed, that
shivered slightly in the afternoon heat as it moved
toward the house, that might yet pass, praise God,
taking only a leaf or a shingle. I still have a few friends
scattered across the state. When we say hello there's
a distance in our eyes as if we had found ourselves in
a field two miles from home.

KANSAS

As she smells the clean sheets the farmer's wife thinks of the 1930's. Wind whips the clothes on the line, blows her dress tight against her heavy legs.

The farmer in his dirty overalls searches through years of broken machinery behind the barn, searches through tall sunflowers, through the nests of rabbits and mice with a wrench in his hand, looking for exactly the right part or one that might do.

Seven skinny cows lie in the mud where the tank overflows. Throughout the long afternoon the wind-mill continues to pump long draughts of cool water.

BARBER SHOP

Someone is helping an old man into the barber shop. The old man is neatly dressed in a blue pinstripe suit that might have been purchased sometime during the Second World War, perhaps for a funeral. He seems unaware of his clothes or his surroundings. Perhaps someone else chose the suit and the clean white shirt and dressed him as one would dress a large doll. He seems to enjoy the warm afternoon sun and seems reluctant to enter the shop. The sun glints on water and steel, on the windows, on scissors and shears and on his great shock of white hair. The voices he hears change and change and he recognizes none of them. The sound of his own name is like a door opening into a dark room— the momentary glare when someone wearing soft-soled shoes enters and leaves again.

ADAM

At first it was okay naming the beasts of the field and the fowls of the air . . . *dog, cat, cow* . . . but it was a time consuming job and after awhile it became boring . . . *slender loris, bridled guillemot* . . . and the insects drove him crazy. Then there were the plants and rocks. Sunrise to sunset, the same thing. He didn't want to just name the things Jehovah had made. He wanted to recombine the elements to make something significant, a creation of his own. He just needed some time off to think, to plan. He wanted a convertible, something sporty, so he could take Eve for a little drive, lovely Eve dressed in her snakeskin miniskirt with the matching bag.

THE POET

He is young and thin with dark hair and a deep, serious voice. He sips his coffee and says "I have found that it is a good idea to check the words you use in a dictionary. I keep a list. Here is the word *meadow*. Since I was a child the word *meadow* always had connotations of peace and beauty. Once I used *meadow* in a poem and as a matter of practice I looked the word up. I found that a *meadow* was a small piece of grassland used to graze animals . . . . Somehow *meadow* was no longer a thing of beauty . . . . "

It is spring. A few cows are grazing in the muddy meadow. There are patches of blackened snow beside the road. It is nearly dark and the ragged poplars at the far end of the meadow have turned black. The animals, the stones, the grass, everything near the earth darkens, and above: the *azure sky*.

AMATEUR ARTIST

He sees that the eyes are wrong. The left eyelid should curve more. He erases and draws the line again. He has no ease with this, no grace, no freedom. It's like work. He wants to get it right. He looks at her photo again and then at the drawing. The drawing looks wrong, too stiff, unnatural. He leaves the eyes and goes to the breasts. He likes this better, the easy graceful sweep of the pencil. Now he sees that the mouth is not right. The paper is nearly worn through in places from erasing and redrawing. How easily everything can go wrong. A misplaced mark becomes a deformity. Another mark and the mood is completely changed. She looks out at him with eyes slightly askew and it's apparent that she is not pleased. Whoever this is.

NO MATTER HOW FAR YOU DRIVE

I sat between Mamma and Daddy.
My sister sat on Mamma's lap.
Daddy drove. Fields, telephone poles. . . .
I watched the sun go down.
"Never look straight at the sun,
it could ruin your eyes."
No matter how far you drive
you can't get to the sun.
I touched the pearly knob
of the gearshift lever
and felt the vibration in my fingers.
It made Daddy nervous.
"Never mess around with that.
You could ruin the car,
cause an accident."
It was dark, the sun gone to China.
Out there in the dark,
fourteen lights. I counted. Fourteen.
Rabbits ran in front of the car
from one black ditch to the other.
I didn't know where we were.
I could see the red light on the dashboard
and the light of Daddy's Lucky Strike
that broke into a million sparks behind us
when he threw it out the window.

TWO

BLACK SPRUCE

Most of us live out our lives
on the edge of something:
bankruptcy, greatness, sanity. . . .
If you could stand back far enough
it might be possible to imagine the forest.
Up close it's trees:
jack pine, balsam, spruce,
alder and popple.
Their dead remain visible,
all tangled up with the living.
Nothing is simplified
by this bucolic setting
but complication becomes more palpable.

In the city it seems no one
treats you as a human being.
The woods, on the other hand,
are full of things that do,
that run if you come too close.

It's lonely.
Who will you talk to?
Who will you invite to your birthday party?
Bears overindulge and fall asleep.
Owls can never remember anyone's name.

If you look a ways down the road
there is a light,
a kind of bluish light,
illuminating a pile of used tires
outside a closed-up gas station.
All around you the black spruce trees
are full of instruction,

pointing this way and that,
waving hello, goodbye.
Here's the road to Brimson, to Wawina.
This way . . . no, here.
Here is the swamp, the river bed,
the glacial esker.
Drive right in.
There's warm porcupine on the blacktop,
cold water in the ditch.
Truly a table is prepared in the wilderness.
When you have walked far enough
you will sit down.

THE MARGINS

Out here between nowhere
and the highway, halfway
to town, in the scrap woods,
where the taxes don't kill you,
are places scraped out of
the popple trees— a well,
septic tank, a mobile home,
broken cars and snowmobiles.
Out here energy
has been transformed into
unstable mass. Alcohol,
divorce, mechanical failure. . .
We live from paycheck to
paycheck, lunging after each
as if climbing a ladder
too large for us, long
abandoned by the angels,
reaching only the high
uncluttered sadness of old age.

FISHING BELOW THE DAM

On summer evenings the working men gather to fish in the swift water below the dam. They sit on the rocks and are silent for the most part, looking into the water and casting again and again. Lines tangle, tackle is lost and a fisherman curses to himself. No one notices. It is simply a part of the routine, like the backs of their wives in bed at night or short words to the children in the morning. Only the water holds their attention, crashing through the spillway with enough force behind it to break a man's back. And the undertow could take you as easily as a bit of fishline and toss you ashore miles downstream. The men shout to be heard above the roar of the water. *ANY LUCK? NO, I JUST GOT HERE.*

AUTOMOBILE REPAIR

It's raining and the car stalls with Mama, the kids
and a full load of laundry inside. At least the warning
lights still work. You raise the hood and find yourself
staring, once again, into the void. Fuel pump? Alter-
nator? The trick is to keep this thing running
without spending any money, akin to making some-
thing from nothing. Thus Jehovah, confronted with
a similar difficulty, simply began assembling the
salvaged parts of the previous universe. Once you
have located the problem you're ready (two or three
cups of coffee will help) to plunge into the mud and
grease. This time it's easy. The wire from the coil to
the distributor has fallen off. It's running again—
bald tires, broken exhaust, rust . . . .

A POOL GAME

They share a cuestick. He breaks, makes the four ball and misses a shot on the six. He puts the cue down carefully, an archbishop surrendering the symbols of the church. He offers a few words of advice on her first shot. She picks up the cue as if it were the Olympic torch and starts off around the table. She puts away the nine, fifteen and the eleven. Bam. Bam. Bam. And this is for you. Pow! The ten. He sits at the bar, bored. He's been playing for so many years. She thinks the game has possibilities, just needs a little work, a little fixing up. She misses a shot on the twelve. He gets up slowly. She is trying to lug a large cement statue of St. Francis into the backyard by herself. He goes to help. Secretly though, it makes him mad. He'll have to fight through the Pacific from island to island again. He's such an old soldier. He picks up his weapon and goes after the deuce and the tray.

THE ALL-NIGHT CHINESE CAFE

Ivor Knutson and his best friend, who was half Indian so everyone called him Chief, were in Ole's Tavern one night arguing which are better, dogs or cats. Both were drunk and when Chief threatened him with a knife, Ivor ran out of the tavern. Half an hour later he was back, firing away with a .22 pistol. He managed not only to kill Chief but Ole, the owner, as well, and to wound three other people before the police arrived. Ivor himself was killed two years later in a prison fight. Those times are referred to now as "the good old days in Ole's Tavern." After the bars closed at night nobody wanted to go home so we went to the all-night Chinese cafe where it was warm and food was cheap. I remember there were bottles of orange soda in the window as a display. The liquid in the bottles had faded over the years so that it was almost clear.

IN THE STREETS

He carries everything he owns in a paper bag. What
are you? A broken alarm clock? A returnable pop
bottle? Once, on this very corner, a man hit him in
the mouth. That's why some of his teeth are missing.
It was drink made that man hit him. He never drinks.
He waits for you every day with his hand out. Every
day without fail. It's a wonder he's still alive. The
coldest days he spends at the public library. But
where does he go at night? The moon is shining now
at four in the afternoon and down here it's all wind
and shadows. In the streets with the blowing snow
and newspapers he carries on the same argument
with his parents, though they have been dead thirty
years. At the mouths of alleys he pauses. . . . He is an
only child. All he wants is his share.

GREEN TOMATO

This morning
after the first frost,
there is a green tomato
among the kleenex,
combs and loose change,
the more usual clutter
on the dresser.
That's the way it is
around here—
things picked up,
put down, lost
or forgotten.
Here is the possibility
of next year's crop,
even more,
in one green tomato.
It makes me smile
to see it there,
newly discovered,
confident and
mysterious as the face
of my young son
who comes to the bedroom
early, ready to play.
There is no point in
my telling you too much
of what makes me
happy or sad.
I did not wake to find,
at this moment,
in this unlikely place,
only my own life.

SOUP

In the yard of her place on a branch of the Knife,
she mixed in the big cast iron pot,
aspen bark, birch root, garlic and beets,
spruce gum, willow twigs, water from the creek,
(tasting slightly of crankcase oil)
road kill, fish heads, cinnamon and leeks.
She added onion and bitter herbs
a touch of sumac, pepper and salt,
withered apples, cabbage and gnarled potatoes.
All day the smoke swirled through bare branches
and the crows overhead circled and dived.
When she took a taste from the big wooden spoon
it wasn't right.

Each ingredient should blend so that each taste
was a reminiscence, sensibly tempered, a joy,
a tonic against the ague and the grippe,
against old age and the grinding cold winter.
It wasn't right this year, flat somehow . . . .
It needed something. But what was it?
Anytime now the guests might arrive.

THE PAINTER

After he has covered
the earth
the painter is ready
to start on the sky.
Beauty requires
constant attention
and, anyway, it's a living.
What color
is the sky today?
Blue.
He stirs the paint,
pours half
into his bucket
and starts
up the ladder
one step
at a time,
slowly.
He climbs
above the trees,
above the cows
grazing in the field,
above the rivers
and mountains.
He leans to one side
and spits—
a long way down.
He doesn't like it much.
He hooks his bucket
to the ladder
and dips his brush.
He makes the first
even stroke.

THE OTHER PEOPLE

One sees them, then forgets. They appear as if in the peripheral vision. They may be what the Irish call "the little people" but they are not really little, a bit smaller perhaps, like large children. . . . I'm not sure. They must inhabit the forest, the night. They sometimes appear in the blue-green light that precedes a thunderstorm. Once I think there were many, but as we humans more and more take over the other places of the world their numbers diminish . . . I think. One is never sure. They appear and the contact brings forgetting, whole blocks of the past vanish from memory. Perhaps this is true for them also, for sometimes they appear startled, unsure. Perhaps nowadays they inhabit basements, warehouses, lockers, scrap woods, the marginal land outside of town. I don't know. They are like us but not exactly. Occasionally one will stand beside you as you wait in line. One of them is busy removing the labels from canned goods in the grocery. Hey! Then you have forgotten, lost the thread of a long, involved argument.

THREE

FISH OUT OF WATER

When he finally landed the fish it seemed so strange, so unlike other fishes he'd caught, so much bigger, more silvery, more important, that he half expected it to talk, to grant his wishes if he returned it to the water. But the fish said nothing, made no pleas, gave no promises. His fishing partner said, "Nice fish, you ought to have it mounted." Other people who saw it said the same thing, "Nice fish. . ." So he took it to the taxidermy shop but when it came back it didn't look quite the same. Still, it was an impressive trophy. Mounted on a big board the way it was, it was too big to fit in the car. In those days he could fit everything he owned into the back of his Volkswagen but the fish changed all that. After he married, a year or so later, nothing would fit in the car. He got a bigger car. Then a new job, children. . . . The fish moved with them from house to house, state to state. All that moving around took its toll on the fish, it began to look worn, a fin was broken off. It went into the attic of the new house. Just before the divorce became final, when he was moving to an apartment, his wife said "Take your goddamn fish." He hung the fish on the wall before he'd un-packed anything else. The fish seemed huge, too big for this little apartment. Boy, it was big. He couldn't imagine he'd ever caught a fish that big.

NORTHERN RIVER

for Phil and Connie

Our map must have been drawn
by an amateur cartographer who,
too anxious to please his readers,
provided imaginary portages
around real rapids.
Muskeg, brush, blackflies and mosquitoes. . .
In one place we had to crash through
a stickery spruce thicket
so dense it must have taken two hours
to go not quite a quarter mile,
to find the river again below the falls.
At a stone-circled backwater
topped with foam and beaver stick flotsam,
we put in finally— weary, scratched up—
slipped out into midstream
and let the water carry the canoe.

We paddle and the canoe moves along
a little faster than the water moves,
and the trees along the shore go past
a little faster than the trees on the hill.
Our rhythmic motion delights us bow and stern.
We say, "It couldn't be better than this!"
"This is perfect, and as long as we follow the river
it's impossible to ever get lost. Right?"

At times the river runs full of intent
between its banks of granite and gabbro
where the tall pines dig into the cracks,
then it falls, turns back on itself and slows
to wander around for hours in the swamp,
muttering the word or two
it has always known.

All that experience good for nothing, finally.
No one remembers the ice age
or much of what happened last week.
One gives up eating raw onions,
and the amorous pursuit of young women
gives way to the cultivation of hair in the ears.
Here on either side—
one-eyed, half-realized—
birch stump, moss and rock,
those shapes that appeared sometimes at night
in your childhood room
and since have waited for your return.
Always lift your hat as you pass
and say, "How do?"

We've wedged ourselves in for the night
among some spruce and balsam
that don't welcome us.
From a nearby blasted white pine
a raven repeats his warning:
"I am a raven. Please do not
violate my personal space."
We grope around in the dark at our feet
for sticks to feed the fire
until fuel and brandy are exhausted
and we've begun our sideways drift to sleep.
The river continues all night
fumbling towards Hudson Bay
in an evolution that goes beyond our participation.
We aren't going that far.
A child said: "A long time ago
people used to be monkeys,
but not you and me."

CLEAR CUT

Short stuff, crew cut,
jack pine and popple,
pulpwood for paper mills;
newspapers and books of poems,
not worth the paper they're printed on.
Something comes up to the tent
but when you look there's nothing.
Silence, the wilderness.
It's annoying.
In this light you can see everything
as a series of lines, planes and angles:
the division of property.
You take the phonograph,
I'll take the records.
You take the car,
I'll take the bus.
You take the baby, I'll take the bathwater.
It's completely practical;
behavior modification.
If your eye offends you,
pluck it out.

THE TENT

Concave on the windward side,
convex on the lee,
it snaps and strains the ropes.
Green nylon not quite the color of the forest,
it is the flag of nothing in particular,
a banner that proclaims
we will not be here very long,
a modest shelter shedding
only the lightest rains.
Like home anywhere,
pitched on an unsheltered point,
the tent wants to fly into the air,
heave sideways into the lake.

EVENING

At dusk the light
chooses carefully
the things it loves;
the water, the white
belly of the fish
the hands of the fisherman,
the bright blade of the knife.

RETURN PORTAGE

First the canoe,
400 rods over a hilly trail
then back for the packs
and the fishing poles
and one last look at the lake.

I wish it would always be like this.
Move up, go back,
pick everything up,
leave nothing
but the pines,
the lake,
the fall afternoon.

PINE SISKINS

All aggression and appetite
they fight for space at the feeder,
ruffling and flapping. Such rudeness
from so delicate a bird.
The weight ratio of brain
to body enhances their capacity
for flight but limits their talent
for reflection and conjecture.
They live out their daily lives
in instinctual confusion,
dropping several seeds
for every one they eat.
It's a folly that serves a need,
feeding a squirrel, rabbit or mouse.
One male sidesteps toward a female
and she sidesteps away
but not very far.
Some unseen signal, some
slight movement or sound, sends
the entire flock into the air;
each bird held perfectly aloft,
unencumbered by engines of faith.

RESTAURANT OVERLOOKING LAKE SUPERIOR

Late afternoon. Only a few old men at the bar,
drinking and talking quietly. Waitresses for the
evening shift begin to arrive. One stands for a moment
at the far end of the dining room and looks out the
window facing the lake. Snow is falling. The lake is
completely obscured, still customers will ask for
tables near the window. A few early diners begin to
arrive, then others. Soon the room is filled with
sounds— people talking, the rattle of dishes, the
waitresses hurrying about. The lake is a great
silence beneath all the noise. In their hurry the
waitresses don't look out the window. Yet they are in
her service, silent a moment as they fill the glasses
with water.

DRIFTWOOD

It is pleasant to lie on the rocky shore in the sun, exposed and open. It's all there; the sound of wind, the sound of waves: the meaningless journal of a lifetime. Nothing is clear, not even the obvious. One loses interest and falls asleep within the water's easy reach.

This driftwood on the beach, dry and bleached white, white as a bone you might say, or white as snow. If an artist (wearing a sweatshirt, blue jeans and tennis shoes without socks) came walking along he might, seeing the possibilities, pick up this piece of driftwood and take it home. Not me. I fling it back in the water.

FOUR

MR. WATKINS

When Mr. Watkins discovered one of the old gods dead in the crawl space under the house he put on his overalls, tied a bandana over his nose and mouth and worked his way beneath the low cobweb covered floor joists on his belly. He planned to drag it out by the heels but as soon as he touched the corpse there was a flash and a pop like a downed powerline. Mr. Watkins' heart stopped and the air smelled of ozone. The resulting fire completely destroyed the house and the garage.

Stray dogs, squirrels, flights of harpies roosting on the t.v. antenna, angels and devils only too ready to spirit you away. . . .

At night Mr. Watkins used to patrol his 75 by 150 foot lot with a flashlight. You could hear his cough, see the light bobbing over the damp grass in summer, over the snowbanks in winter. Mr. Watkins was an old man and forgot things easily but he knew where the property lines were drawn and, by god, if you don't know that you don't know anything.

VIBRATION

The window pane vibrates at a constant, barely audible frequency. One doesn't notice it at first, but it can be quite annoying once you become aware of it. The water in this glass vibrates when I set it on the table— waves in a miniature ocean. The glass vibrates; therefore the table is moving. Put your fingers here or there and you can feel it. And the floor. Perhaps there is some large machine nearby working day and night, some tremendous project that never gets completed. If you look long enough at anything— the house next door, the leafless ash tree, the old woman in the ratty fur walking her overweight dog— you can see the slight blurring, a kind of blue-white outline, an uncertainty, a sadness as each thing separates itself from the air.

THE WRISTWATCH

In the morning, after he'd dressed, he looked for his wristwatch on the nightstand and discovered that it was missing. He looked in the drawer and on the floor, under the bed. It was nowhere to be seen. He looked in the bathroom, checked the pockets of his jacket, his pants. He looked downstairs in the kitchen, the living room. He went out to check the car. He went to the basement and looked through the laundry. He went back upstairs and looked everywhere again. He said "Have you seen my watch?" to his wife, to his children. "I'm sure I left it on the nightstand." He became obsessed with finding the watch. He removed all the drawers from the dresser one by one, emptying their contents onto the bedroom floor. Impossible. Someone must have come in the night and taken it. A watch thief, who with great stealth and cunning, disdaining silverware, jewelry, cameras, fine art, money, had made his way to the bedside and stolen his Timex wristwatch. Perhaps his wife had, for years, been harboring some secret grudge and finally, unable to bear it any longer, had taken revenge by flushing his watch down the toilet. Maybe his seven-year-old was supporting a drug habit. One thing was certain: nothing . . . nothing was the way he'd thought it had been.

CLOUD ATLAS

—Eh! qu'aimes-tu donc, extraordinaire étranger?
—J'aime les nuages... les nuages qui passent...
là-bas... là-bas... les merveilleux nuages!

—Baudelaire

I. Cumulus

One lives in the world
more quietly, sometimes, than one would like.
And yes, beyond this world is another.
One lives with that world too,
as with a crazy uncle
who comes downstairs occasionally
for whiskey and cigarettes,
then it's back up to his room
where he's working on a plan
of significance to the world at large,
thinking. . . .
It's quiet.
He's right though,
beyond this second world is yet another.
World piles on world in a compact and towering mass
that, with its domes and canyons,
resembles a cauliflower
or the human brain.

Each moment, though it passes silently,
is a turmoil of emotions,
our smallest actions driven by workings
more complex than those of a watch
but less precise.

46

(I lean toward you over the pina coladas
as our converstation drifts from
the international monetary crisis
to your favorite music.)
We expect certain grace with all this energy
the way the *Arethusa*, under Liberian registry,
slides across the oily water to her berth
easily, swiftly . . .
a little too swiftly perhaps. . . . Full Astern!
White water boils up behind,
seagulls fly away. . . .
Too late.
There will be an investigation,
the captain relieved of his command.

We give names to the winds aloft
and expect them to arrange everything.
Because of Love a man will leave his home
and spend the rest of his life in Pittsburgh.
It's frightening.
One thing leads to another.

II. Stratus

Everywhere you look are the poor, the old and sick,
those who must count the cost of everything,
each tooth, each hair numbered,
each icy step a risk,
those for whom one and one and one
add up to nothing, no horizon,
a shuffling walk from bed
to window where the muted light
plays on the building next door.

Today air and water have fused,
no lake, no sky, no horizon . . .
an apartment wall.
A Kline poster, books, cinder blocks and
boards,
teapot, frying pan, coffee cups . . .
the dishes pile up in the sink.
The faucet drips, drips
as grey afternoon ticks into evening.
A woman moves in, perhaps,
bringing curtains, a rug,
a couple of geckos.
But you, preoccupied,
listen to the careful tick, tick,
considering the possible combinations,
waiting for the tumblers to fall.

The colors are black and white
or combinations thereof.
The answers are yes and no,
yes no yes no no no and yes
or maybe
when seen from a distance.
From here it is possible
to think in the grandest terms
yet someone walking just behind you
has disappeared
between one and zero.

III. Cirrus

It seems to me you enjoyed
shattering the fine bone china
though the focus of our discussion
escapes me. Perhaps there was
a wisp of hair that curled
in front of your ear that you
brushed back as you spoke.
I've forgotten because I kissed you,
probably, and took your hand awhile.
Beneath that translucent skin
the tiny veins branch
to invisible capillaries:
the ancient delta culture bred
to a fine nervous instability.
Perhaps so much detail
left us confused, confounded
by a superfluity of information:
shoe sizes, opinions about Nietzsche. . . .

One wearies of matters of substance.
I recommend those moments
that, without reason, last a lifetime:
the girl on the shore
brushing her teeth as we sailed away,
a glimpse of a face, a shoulder
in a doorway;
moments like music,
truth untroubled by meaning.
Of course, there's not,
at this altitude, enough oxygen
for a swallow, let alone
a family of four.

That first glimpse, as the plane turned,
of the Sangre de Cristos
with their lacework of snow
set against the western sky,
patterns repeated in cloud, in sand,
in sun on water all seemed, somehow,
like mileposts on the true way,
indicators of something that
would finally reveal itself.
Yet, at any moment the wind
could peel back the pie-crust aluminum
exposing the sham, the skein of wire,
the ridiculous construct of kitchenware
and string that could not,
under any circumstance, allow for flight. . . .

Still, we seem to be moving right along.

UNFORTUNATE LOCATION

In the front yard there are three big white pines, older than anything in the neighborhood except the stones. Magnificent trees that toss their heads in the wind like the spirited black horses of a troika. It's hard to know what to do, tall dark trees on the south side of the house, an unfortunate location, blocking the winter sun. Dark and damp. Moss grows on the roof, the porch timbers rot and surely the roots have reached the old bluestone foundation. At night, in the wind, a tree could stumble and fall killing us in our beds. The needles fall year after year making an acid soil where no grass grows. We rake the fallen debris, nothing to be done, we stand around with sticks in our hands. Wonderful trees.

GHOSTS

Everything about them is vague. They drift about somewhat resentful that no one recognizes their presence. But how could anyone since ghosts don't really exist? Their tricks to gain attention, moaning and rattling chains don't amount to much in a world inured to terrors. Now and then one will update his work and honk the car horn until the battery goes dead. No use. It's dismissed as curious but trivial, another of life's little irritations. They have a persistant feeling, never quite articulated, that one day they will awaken to life again. Like someone always on the verge of making it big. Something unspecific, winning the lottery perhaps, or an inheritance. When they manage to focus for an instant on a thought, the triumph of that instant becomes equated with the deed. As when, having duly noted that the cobwebs need to be cleaned from a particular corner, I proceed complacently to other activities. Centuries of woolgathering pass in what seems to them only moments. The earth changes until nothing is recognizable and still this vague longing moves upon the face of the deep.

BANANAS

Bananas, badly cooked meat,
candy at the carnival,
or flies in conjunction with the heat
caused Joey Stoner to die of polio . . .
or swimming in Skeleton creek
with those nigger kids,
old Mrs. Clark said, she seen him. . . .

You have to take care to prevent
slump shoulders, flat feet.
If the baby sleeps on his back
the back of his head will be flat.
One has to make constant small corrections,
keeping the time
and the position of the stars.

That light that comes to us
across billions of miles of space
is only a reminder
of something that happened a long time ago.
In the split-second before hydrogen formed,
when a decision was called for,
nobody did a thing.

Introspection and examination,
your own fooling and fussing,
push the electrons around
so when you return home late,
tiptoe down the hall, shoes in hand,
suddenly there's a lampcord, a rollerskate. . . .

Outside, the summer insects
orbit the single light on the corner
and from far down the block
a child calls out in the dark
"You can't get me. You can't get me."

ON AGING

There are no compensations for growing old. Certainly not wisdom. And one gave up anticipating heaven long ago. Perhaps there is a kind of anesthesia resulting from short-term memory loss, from diminished libido, from apathy and fatigue which is mistaken for patience.

The rich can afford to grow old gracefully but the flesh of the poor shows each defeat like a photographic plate that records the movement of the planets and the stars and the rotation of the earth. Eyesight fails and hearing, the skin wrinkles and cracks, the bones twist, the muscles degenerate. . . . It takes all morning to open a can of soup.

The world collapses inward. Memory is no recompense. The past is fiction, a story of interest only to the young. There is only, as there always was, the moment. The instant, which, when you become aware of it, is blinding as the flash when someone snaps a picture of you blowing out the candles.

RESTORATION

The idea is to restore one of these Victorian monsters
to its original grandeur— with a modern kitchen and
bathroom, of course. Low-cost home improvement
loans are available.

In the old days things were built to last. . . giant oak
timbers imbedded in granite, cast iron cogwheels
and worm gears that drove certain adjuncts of the
heavenly spheres. Pieces remain but no one remem-
bers exactly what they were for.

In those days fuel was cheap. One could heat several
rooms with an afternoon of hard thought on the
subject of free will. Inside one of the cupboards is a
special small door to the outside, like a pet door, so
the cold can come in.

With rotten timbers, plaster falling all around, this
job requires a will of iron, like the border fence, bent
and rusted near the ground, that still hangs on like
God and empire. Let's paint this place in true colors
of the period, dark green and red, repression and
madness. An excess of quiet ostentatiousness.

WINTER CLOTHES

We come in puffing and stamping— goose down, wool, heavy boots, mittens, scarf. . . . Winter clothes bear the same relationship to the body as the body does to the soul, a sort of cocoon where those you thought you knew are changed beyond recognition. . . . We greet each other with awkward affection, like bears. Someone removes a glove and extends a pale hand.

His hand on the green silk of her dress, lightly, on the small of her back, sleepwalking there in the forest. And on the inside, the ravelled thread ends, untidy windfall where the hunter walks to flush the startled bird. . . and afterwards silence . . . a handful of feathers, like letters from another woman found in a bankbox after his death, casting a whole new light on the subject.

When you get to the end there is always one more thing. The mind insists that we live on after death whether we walk stiffly in bodies cold and drained of color or drift like tall columns of mist across the northern lakes, taller than we were in life but no more substantial.

We must look inside to find the answer, pulling the layers away like the leaves of an artichoke. And the answer is incorrect.

WIND CHIME

Eventually someone will get sick of this clatter and will tie up the strings or remove the whole contraption. This instrument was meant for subtler sounds, silence and overtones, only the hint of a breeze, days in which the phone does not ring even once, long afternoons that fade into twilight with a single star there in the bell-clear western sky. One sighs and lays the book aside. . . . But the wind is unrelenting. It must have been like this long ago, a single sound over and over until at last someone sitting alone in the early dark became aware of it and realized what it means to be alive.

Louis Jenkins' poems have been published in *American Poetry Review*, *Boston Review*, *Kenyon Review*, *Poetry East*, *Virginia Quarterly Review* and other magazines and anthologies. In addition he has published three poetry chapbooks and in 1987, The Eighties Press and Ally Press published his first full-length collection, *An Almost Human Gesture*. Mr. Jenkins was awarded a Bush Foundation Fellowship for poetry in 1979 and again in 1984. He was a 1987 winner of the Loft-McKnight Award for Poetry. Louis Jenkins lives in Duluth, Minnesota with his wife and son.